What the Donner Party?

by Ben Hubbard

illustrated by Tim Foley

Penguin Workshop

For Leti, my number-one fan—BH

PENGUIN WORKSHOP
An imprint of Penguin Random House LLC, New York

First published in the United States of America by Penguin Workshop,
an imprint of Penguin Random House LLC, New York, 2023

Visit us online at penguinrandomhouse.com.

Library of Congress Control Number: 2023020958

Printed in the United States of America

ISBN 9780593520741 (paperback)   10 9 8 7 6 5 4 3 2 1 WOR
ISBN 9780593520758 (library binding)   10 9 8 7 6 5 4 3 2 1 WOR

Contents

What Was
the Donner Party?

In late October 1846, one last push was all that
was needed. One last push for the men, women,
and children to reach the mountain summit—
its highest peak—and cross to the other
side. But the pass to the summit
was a steep slope covered with
several feet of snow.
It was too deep
for wagons.

The group would have to gather their most precious possessions and walk. There were arguments about what to take. Men wanted to bring boxes of tobacco; women insisted on taking rolls of cloth. A man named Charles Stanton urged them to hurry. If more snow fell, the pass would be blocked. Then there would be no way over the mountain. They had to seize their chance now. Finally, in the early afternoon, the group set out.

Stanton took two Miwok guides, Luis and Salvador, to scout ahead. They were soon pushing through chest-high snow. With great effort, the men reached the summit. There, they stood high on the Sierra Nevada, a mountain range running through western North America. Below, a vast swath of California stretched out before them. This is the place the group known as the Donner Party had traveled thousands of miles to reach. Their journey from the eastern

Luis and Salvador lead Charles Stanton

United States had been one of severe hardships. They had endured treacherous mountains, suffocating desert heat, and an almost impassable shortcut. Now, after six exhausting months, the end was in sight. One last push was all that was needed.

Carrying their children and sacks of their belongings, the group struggled in the deep snow. They stepped up and over the top layer only to sink down into it with the next step. Tired and hungry, the group inched forward.

Stanton, Luis, and Salvador tracked back down the pass to help the group to the summit.

But to their dismay, everyone had stopped. The group was sitting in the snow, seemingly unable to move. Someone had set fire to a pine tree covered with resin. Hands were being warmed in the glow. Above them, the moon shone as the light faded. Luis warned that a ring around the moon meant more snow was coming.

More snow would surely block the pass ahead of them. If they were to reach the summit, they must leave now. Stanton pleaded with the group to stand up and start walking. They were so close. Just one last push . . .

CHAPTER 1
Westward Ho!

The town of Springfield, Illinois, was alive with activity in April 1846. Families in covered wagons pulled by oxen filled the muddy streets.

They were emigrants—people who relocate to settle elsewhere in the hope of better lives—on their way west to California and Oregon. These territories were seen as places where dreams could come true, with warm weather, fertile soil, and enough space for everyone. Thousands of families in the eastern United States made the journey west in the 1840s. They traveled in covered wagons towed by oxen. They were also known as pioneers.

The settlers from Illinois would not be traveling alone. They were joining a train of over five hundred wagons in Independence, Missouri, around three hundred miles west. The two wagon trains would meet up and make the 2,500-mile journey together. It would take six months, across prairies, deserts, and mountain ranges. They were leaving in the spring so they did not become trapped by snow during the winter. They had to plan their journey west carefully.

Westward Expansion

The United States of America was established in 1776 by people living in the thirteen original colonies along the East Coast. The nation more than doubled in 1803 when President Thomas Jefferson bought the Louisiana Purchase (the land from the Mississippi River to the Rocky Mountains) from the French government. Jefferson then ordered Meriwether Lewis and William Clark to explore this new western territory and find a route to the Pacific Ocean. They met over fifty native tribes on their journey, many of whom provided the explorers with important supplies, information, and hospitality.

Soon afterward, pioneers began moving west to settle in this new land. Between 1840 and 1850, many of these pioneers were white farmers who had been born in the East. After the Transcontinental Railroad was finished in 1869, new immigrants from northern Europe also migrated west. German, Scandinavian, and Irish immigrants were common among them. This movement of people in the United States was known as the Westward Expansion.

The Springfield families included the Reeds and Donners. They each had different reasons for emigrating to California. George and Tamzene Donner and their five children were farmers who wanted to leave rising crop prices and infertile land behind. California promised vast green pastures. George's brother Jacob, his wife, Elizabeth, and their seven children were also with them.

George Donner

James and Margaret Reed

James and Margaret Reed ran a successful mill and a furniture business in Springfield. But Margaret suffered from headaches that James thought the California climate might cure. To make the journey as comfortable as possible for his family, James built a luxurious wagon called the "Pioneer Palace Car."

Most covered wagons were made simply from wood with a canvas roof. The driver sat on

a wooden bench at the front to steer the oxen.
Passengers got in and out from an opening in
the back. But the Pioneer Palace Car had a side
door, a wood-burning stove, cushioned seats, and
bunks for sleeping. The Pioneer Palace Car was
a marvel but also heavy—it took a team of eight

The Pioneer Palace Car

oxen to pull it instead of the usual four.

Oxen were the best animals for towing wagons long-distance. Unlike mules and horses that only ate grass, oxen could eat sagebrush and other shrubs. They were also less likely to run away

Oxen

than mules and horses—but they were slower. Fifteen miles a day by oxen was considered good progress. This meant the families could walk alongside their wagons, which most men did. Others rode horses and mules, while men called "teamsters" were hired to drive the wagons themselves. Including their teamsters, the

Springfield families made up thirty-two people. They became known as the Donner Party. A *party* is another name for a group.

Each family had three wagons. The first wagon was for living in. The second wagon was like a moving truck, with the family's furniture and other possessions. The third wagon carried supplies for the journey: food, clothes, cooking utensils, and tools. A guidebook at the time suggested travelers take the following quantities of food: 150 pounds of bacon; 200 pounds of flour; 20 pounds of sugar, 10 pounds of coffee, and 10 pounds of salt. Cornmeal, cured meat, dried beans, tea, pickles, mustard, and dried fruit were also suggested.

The Donner Party reached Independence, Missouri, on May 10. The town was buzzing with last-minute preparations. Two days later, the wagon train would "jump off" into the prairie land of what is modern-day Kansas. George Donner's youngest daughter, Eliza, later wrote:

"[We] took a last look at Independence, turned our backs to the morning sun, and became pioneers indeed to the far West."

Eliza Donner

CHAPTER 2
Jumping Off

After setting off from Independence, Missouri, the wagon train entered the Great Plains. Mostly flat, dry prairie land, the Great Plains stretch across ten modern US states. The wagons traveled through this territory on the Oregon Trail, a track well-worn by previous wagon trains. The pioneers' progress was steady and the weather fair. Eliza Donner later reported "fields of May blossoms musical with the hum of bees and the songs of birds." The families soon settled into a regular daily schedule.

At dawn, a trumpeter roused sleepers from their beds. Breakfasts of coffee, bacon, salt pork, and mushy cornmeal were prepared over campfires. Every meal would include dried fruit to prevent scurvy, the disease caused by a lack of vitamin C. The grazing oxen were then hitched up to the wagons. All going well, they would roll onto the trail by 7:30 a.m. each day.

Women and children helped the men drive the oxen, as well as mended clothes and performed other chores in the wagons. The oxen moved so slowly that there was time to visit other wagons. Some said it was possible to stop and write a letter by the side of the trail and easily catch up to their wagon afterward.

The group would stop at twelve o'clock for lunch. This was called "nooning." They ate cold food, such as cured meat, pickles, baked beans, and coffee. After resuming the journey, the families usually stopped between four and six o'clock to pitch camp. Wagons formed a circle, or "corral," with the animals inside. This formation

offered some protection against attacks by wolves or American Indian warriors who didn't want the white settlers to cross their land. Sentries with rifles would stand guard.

The Displacement of American Indians

When European settlers came to North America in the sixteenth century, the land was populated by millions of Indigenous people of many different nations, or "Indians," as they were called. But throughout the Westward Expansion in the 1800s, American Indians were forced to relocate to land on the Great Plains, called "Indian Territory" by white settlers, during the 1830s and 1840s. Many American Indian people were imprisoned and murdered during their forced relocation. Some tribal nations resisted and fought back. Settlers traveling west often feared American Indians and thought of them as "savages." In reality, some nations, such as the Paiute, could be both friendly and hostile, while others such as the Kaw and Washoe helped westward-bound pioneers in many ways.

Washoe family

For the most part, evenings were spent relaxing around the campfire. When hunting was possible, fish and fresh meat might be on the dinner menu. After dinner, there was often music and dancing. But there was always work to do, too. Repairs would be made and water and wood collected.

The Great Plains' bison, also sometimes called buffalo, were hunted for their meat. James Reed shot an elk and two buffalo, and he was considered the best hunter of the group. His daughter Virginia Reed noted that "the meat of the young buffalo is excellent." She and the other children would collect dried buffalo dung, called "chips." Buffalo chips made very good campfire fuel. Buffalo were plentiful in North America at that time—some estimates place the number between twenty and sixty million.

Before long, the wagon train rolled on from Kansas into Nebraska. On the dry, dusty trail, the weather became unseasonably cold and then unbearably hot. Inside the wagons, the temperature could reach one hundred degrees. As the heat took its toll, progress became slower. The Donner Party was already at the back of the larger wagon train. And every day, the group fell farther behind. The Donner Party was going too slow. Every day, they seemed to pitch camp earlier and leave later. Some days, they only traveled eight

Edwin Bryant

miles, or even four. "I am beginning to feel alarmed at the tardiness of our movements and fearful that winter will find us in the snowy mountains of California," journalist Edwin Bryant wrote in his diary.

In June, the group snaked along the Platte River, and crossed from Nebraska to Wyoming. The river was shallow and muddy, and it did not make for good drinking water. The landscape was changing, too. Large rocky landmarks rose up from the horizon, with names such as Courthouse Rock, Chimney Rock, and Independence Rock.

Chimney Rock

In Wyoming, Virginia Reed came across a sight she had been fearing: Sioux warriors in full battle gear. In Kansas, the pioneers had been helped over a river by the friendly Kaw Nation. But now they saw the Sioux preparing to fight their enemies, the Blackfoot and Crow. Virginia recorded the moment in her diary: "Some of our company became alarmed, and the rifles were cleaned out and loaded, to let the warriors see that we were prepared to fight; but the Sioux never showed any inclination to disturb us."

Instead, the Sioux became very interested in Virginia Reed's pony, Billy. They offered to buy Billy in exchange for precious buffalo robes and horses of their own. Although Billy was not for sale, James Reed invited the Sioux warriors for breakfast. Afterward, the settlers eagerly struck out for their next stopping point, Fort Laramie. It was here, however, that their fate would be forever changed.

CHAPTER 3
Forts, Friends, and Foes

Along the trail, James Reed often consulted a guidebook called *The Emigrants' Guide to Oregon and California*. It was written by a young lawyer named Lansford Hastings who had already traveled west and considered himself an expert guide. Unfortunately, he was no expert. But he did have ambitious plans. Hastings wanted to be "president

Lansford Hastings

of California." To do this, he needed more people to move to California. Then California could declare itself an independent US state. (At that time the land belonged to Mexico.) To help his plan along,

Hastings promoted a shortcut to California. He called it the Hastings Cutoff.

The cutoff was a more direct route west. It meant leaving the Oregon Trail in what is now Utah and crossing the Great Salt Lake Desert. However, even though he recommended taking this shortcut, Hastings had little knowledge of it himself. He had certainly never attempted to cross it in a wagon. But he was so eager for wagon trains to move through the cutoff trail that he made himself available to personally guide them over it. In July 1846, Lansford Hastings was waiting near his cutoff at Fort Bridger for just this task.

Three hundred miles to the east, the Donner Party was a full week behind the main wagon train. Tired and dusty, the group was only just reaching Fort Laramie in eastern Wyoming. There, they could rest, resupply, and catch up on news from the trail.

Forts of the West

Built as military bases, trading posts, and supply centers, forts were a welcome stop for weary travelers in the American West. In the mid-1800s, the US government ordered military forts to be built along the Oregon Trail to ensure the safety of wagon trains.

Fort Laramie was the second fort to be built for this purpose. Constructed from wooden stockades and adobe bricks, a fort provided a secure place to sleep and eat as well as to purchase supplies. The other main forts on the trail west were Fort Kearny, Fort Bridger, Fort Hall, Fort Boise, Fort Vancouver, and Sutter's Fort.

Fort Laramie

The Rocky Mountains

Fort Laramie was constructed with high walls and an inner courtyard at the foot of the Rocky Mountains. Stretching for over three thousand miles, the Rockies form the longest mountain range in North America. The people who stopped at Fort Laramie were traders, fur trappers, American Indians, US soldiers, settlers heading west, and mountain men—explorers who lived in the wilderness. By chance, one such mountain man staying at the fort at this time was James Clyman, an ex-soldier and former friend of James Reed.

After dinner, Reed and Clyman sat by the fire and talked into the night. Clyman, who was one of the few people who had actually traveled through the Hastings Cutoff, said that Lansford Hastings could not be trusted and that wagons could not cross the shortcut. Clyman pleaded with Reed not to leave the Oregon Trail, saying, "Take the regular wagon track and never leave it—it is barely possible to get through if you follow it—and it may be impossible if you don't." But James Reed disagreed, saying, "There is a nigher [nearer] route, and it is of no use to take such a roundabout course." Reed would not change his mind. When the Donner Party headed out a few days later, Reed worked to convince the others to take the ill-advised shortcut. And then, as if by magic, a rider appeared on the trail. He carried a letter from none other than Lansford Hastings. The letter said that Hastings was waiting at Fort Bridger to personally help them across his cutoff.

The Donner Party put the matter to a vote. Tamzene Donner and others voiced their concern. Eliza Donner later wondered how they could "confide in the statement of a man of whom they knew nothing, but was probably some selfish

Tamzene Donner

adventurer." However, women and children were not allowed to vote. In the end, the men chose to take the Hastings Cutoff.

On July 20, the wagon train reached a fork in the road. To the north, the Oregon Trail continued. To the west lay a trail called the Parting of the Ways. The Donner Party turned onto this trail, and several other families joined them.

The Parting of the Ways

These families included: Margaret and Patrick Breen and their seven children; Franklin and Elizabeth Graves with their nine children and a daughter's husband; Levinah Murphy and her extended family, which included the Fosters and Pikes; William and Eleanor Eddy and their two children; and Lewis and Elisabeth Keseberg and their two children. There were also several single men, including Charles Stanton, Patrick Dolan, and John Snyder.

Margaret and Patrick Breen

More people meant that there would be safety in numbers but also more voices to disagree with one another. It was decided a leader should be elected. It was clear that James Reed already considered himself the leader of the group. But some considered him self-centered and arrogant.

Instead, George Donner was elected to lead the group, which now became known as the Donner Party. This wagon train now consisted of twenty-three wagons and eighty-seven people: twenty-nine men, fifteen women, and forty-three children.

Fort Bridger

Their last stop before the Hastings Cutoff was Fort Bridger. The Donner Party rolled into the fort on July 24. It was not an impressive sight. Inside a rough stockade of wooden poles that acted as a makeshift outer fence were "two or three miserable log cabins, rudely constructed and bearing but a faint resemblance to habitable houses," according to Edwin Bryant, who had written about Fort Bridger when he had passed through the fort only a few days earlier.

Bryant had been a part of the larger wagon train from Independence. Now, he had scouted out the cutoff ahead. The news was not good: Bryant had found the cutoff nearly impassable. He wrote a letter urging Reed not to take the cutoff and left it with Jim Bridger, of Fort Bridger, hoping he would give it to James Reed.

When Reed arrived at Fort Bridger, he expected to find Lansford Hastings waiting. Instead, the Donner Party was welcomed in by Jim Bridger and his partner, Louis Vasquez. They told Reed that the cutoff was "a fine level road, with plenty of water and grass" and that it would reduce the journey west by four hundred miles.

Jim Bridger   Louis Vasquez

Jim Bridger never gave Edwin Bryant's letter of warning to Reed. And Bridger and Vasquez were lying about the level road ahead. The Oregon Trail had taken potential customers away from Fort Bridger, so they weren't earning much money. They needed the Donner Party to buy supplies from them. These included moccasins and buffalo robes that the families would need in the cold Sierra Nevada. With no other forts around for competition, Bridger and Vasquez kept their prices high. They had to recommend the cutoff as the best route in order to keep wagon trains moving through Fort Bridger.

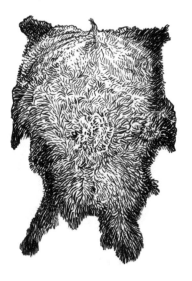

Moccasins

Buffalo robe

The Donner Party did not realize it at the time, but they had been lied to. The only positive was the plentiful grass and fresh water to feed their exhausted livestock. On July 31, the party started along the alternate route of the Hastings Cutoff.

CHAPTER 4
The Hastings Cutoff

Disaster struck only a few miles into the Hastings Cutoff passage. The teenaged Edward Breen fell off his horse, breaking his leg between the ankle and knee. A rider galloped back to Fort Bridger to find a doctor.

He returned with "a rough looking man with long whiskers" who unraveled a bundle containing a short saw and a long knife. The only solution, the man said, was to cut Edward's leg off before infection set in. Edward pleaded with his parents to prevent the amputation. Finally, Edward's parents gave in and sent the man away with five dollars for his trouble. Luckily, Edward's leg healed over the weeks that followed.

The trail, which had been flat and easy at first, was becoming narrow, windy, and steep. Eventually the wagons reached Weber Canyon, a

Weber Canyon

rocky passage into the Wasatch Mountains that they would have to cross. There was no clear path ahead. But there was a note attached to a sagebrush.

This note was from Lansford Hastings. It urged the pioneers to stop, as the way ahead was impassable. It suggested riders be sent forth to find Hastings so he could come back to help. James Reed and Charles Stanton immediately rode out from the rest of the group.

The two riders crossed the Wasatch Mountains

and found Hastings camped on the other side.
He had just helped another wagon train across
the mountains. It had not gone well. They had to
double-team their oxen (hitch two teams to each
wagon) to pull the wagons over a nearly vertical

slope. Several wagons had been lost.

Reed had never met Hastings, the man he had trusted with the fate of the Donner Party. Now he explained that the entire group was waiting for Hastings to lead them across his cutoff. Hastings agreed to ride back to show the pioneers a better route. On the way back, however, Hastings changed his mind. From a nearby peak, he pointed out a possible new route to Reed. And then he departed. The Donner Party was on its own.

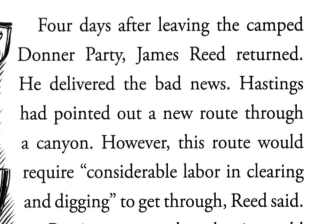 Four days after leaving the camped Donner Party, James Reed returned. He delivered the bad news. Hastings had pointed out a new route through a canyon. However, this route would require "considerable labor in clearing and digging" to get through, Reed said.

But it was soon clear that it would require much more than that. As the wagons pulled up to the canyon entrance, it was obvious that no one had ever passed through. Before them was a dense forest of brush, cottonwood, aspen, willow, maple, and oak trees. The men went to work. Each tree had to be felled and then dragged away to clear a path. It was a backbreaking job that took six days to complete. Then, at the end of the canyon, a massive boulder lay in the way. To pass this obstacle, oxen had to be double-teamed to drag each wagon up the slope around the giant rock.

Finally, after nearly a month, the Donner Party crossed the canyon. "Worn with travel and greatly discouraged, we reached the shore of the Great Salt Lake," Virginia Reed wrote. The shore of that lake is actually a four-thousand-square-mile dry desert that used to be part of the Great Salt Lake just above it. Now evaporated, only a salty top layer is left. The Great Salt Lake Desert stretched out for miles in front of the group.

Before they entered the desert, Tamzene Donner noticed some paper scraps scattered on the ground. She pieced the scraps together and read what was written there. It said: "Two days—two nights—hard driving—cross desert—reach water." It was a note from Lansford Hastings.

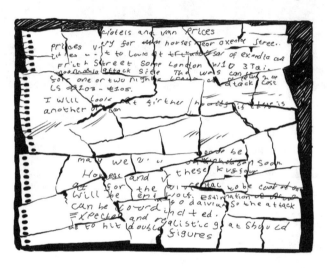

There was nothing to do but to keep moving forward. They filled barrels with water from a nearby stream and picked as much grass for their oxen as they could. It was evening when they struck out. The moonlight sparkled on the salt crystals that crunched beneath their feet and the wheels of their wagons. As the night wore on, the desert became black and the air bitterly cold. As dawn broke, the Donner Party kept walking.

In the distance lay a mountain called Pilot Peak, the source of a freshwater spring.

As the group walked, they narrowed their

eyes against the blinding glare of the sun.
Wind blew the powdery salt around them. The
salt burned their skin and made the air taste
metallic. The sun baked the salty desert into
a hard crust but cooked the moisture below
it into a thick soup. Soon the wagons were
sinking down into this salty muck. The oxen,
already dehydrated, strained to pull the wagons
through. Mules sank to their knees and then
kicked up salt dust as they pulled themselves out.
Two days went on in this way: baking heat during

the day and frigid cold at night. Before long, most of the group had run out of water. Some soaked rags in what remained to put over the tongues of their oxen. Several oxen had already died of thirst.

James Reed rode ahead. He made it to the Pilot Peak spring and returned with fresh water. But he found that several of his oxen had run off into the desert. Without enough oxen to tow their wagons, many of the Reeds' possessions would have to be abandoned. Virginia's pony, Billy, sat down and refused to get up. Leaving Billy behind, the Reeds pushed forward.

After almost a week, the Donner Party reached the other side of the Great Salt Lake Desert and

rested by the Pilot Peak Spring. It took another four days for the group to exit the cutoff path and join the California Trail taken by the rest of the wagons heading west. Normally there would have been other wagon trains on the trail, but they had long since passed. The main wagon train the Donner Party had split from at the Parting of the Ways would soon reach its destination.

Taking the cutoff had been a disaster for the Donner Party. It had added a month to their

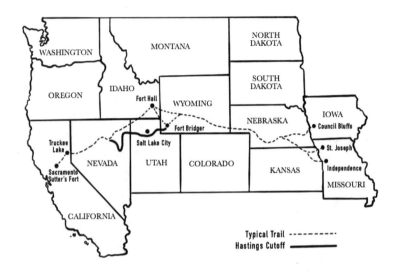

Typical Trail ----------
Hastings Cutoff ━━━━━

journey and an extra 125 miles; thirty-six oxen had died or escaped; several wagons had been abandoned; and there was now not enough food to get the group to California.

Charles Stanton volunteered to ride to Sutter's Fort in California and return with supplies. This gave those in the Donner Party some hope, but most felt devastated. Many blamed Lansford Hastings for their trouble; others blamed James Reed. "Anguish and dismay now filled all hearts. Husbands bowed their heads, appalled at the situation of their families," Eliza Donner wrote.

CHAPTER 5
Into the Mountains

The Donner Party followed the California Trail along the Humboldt River, in what is now the state of Nevada. It was already October, and the daylight hours were getting shorter. So, too, were tempers among the travelers. On October 5, anger exploded when the wagons of James Reed and John Snyder became entangled.

Snyder flew into a rage and began whipping Reed's oxen. When Reed stepped in, Snyder struck him in the head. With blood running down his face, Reed pulled out his knife and stabbed Snyder near his collarbone. John Snyder dropped down dead.

Several families demanded justice. Lewis Keseberg said Reed should be hanged. Margaret Reed begged for her husband's life. In the end, it was agreed Reed should be banished from the group. After helping to bury Snyder, Reed mounted a horse and rode away. The Donner Party headed out once again.

Lewis Keseberg

The trail by the Humboldt River was hot and dusty, and there were few trees to provide shelter from the baking sun. The water in the river was brown, muddy, and not good for drinking. Then, a new danger appeared: the threat of a group of hostile Paiute.

Paiute warriors

One night, two Paiute stole two of the settlers' oxen. A few nights later, all the Graveses' horses were stolen. Another night, nineteen oxen went missing; twenty-one more were then either stolen or shot with arrows. Now there were scarcely enough oxen to tow the wagons. The Graveses and Eddys had to abandon their wagons and continue on foot. Margaret Reed had already abandoned the famed Pioneer Palace Car. Worse still, there were fewer oxen to provide precious meat if needed.

The party finally reached the Truckee River at the foot of the Sierra Nevada. Lying between Nevada and California, the Sierra Nevada is over 250 miles long. Reaching the Truckee River

Truckee River

gave the travelers a rare moment of happiness. There were plenty of trees, green grass, and cool, clean water. Then, there appeared an even more cheering sight. Charles Stanton emerged at the head of a mule train carrying food and supplies. These goods had been provided by John Sutter of Sutter's Fort in California. Sutter had also sent two Miwok guides, Luis and Salvador, to help guide the group. There was good news for the Reed family, too: James had made it safely to Sutter's Fort.

The weary pioneers pushed up the mountain until they reached a valley containing Truckee Lake. Above the icy-blue lake was a steep pass between large boulders. The pass led to the mountain summit and the trail to California. Sutter's Fort lay less than ninety miles away. But snow was already on the ground. The group needed to cross the mountain immediately.

Sutter's Fort

The Donner Party then divided into two groups: those who would cross the pass, and those who would rest before attempting it. After arguments about what to take, Charles Stanton, Luis, and Salvador led the Reeds, the Eddys, the Graveses, and the Kesebergs forward. But snow quickly became a problem. "The farther we went up, the deeper the snow got," Virginia Reed wrote.

At a point below the summit, the exhausted group paused for breath. Stanton, Luis, and Salvador pushed ahead to the summit. They crunched the snow down into a path as they went up. The group behind them could simply follow the path to cross the summit.

But when the men came back down, the entire group had stopped. They sat around a burning pine tree and did not move. Stanton pleaded with them: This might be their last chance to cross the mountain this winter. But it was no use. Some had already dug out beds in the snow and laid down blankets and buffalo hides. Before long, everyone had fallen asleep. Above them, the burning pine tree popped and crackled before extinguishing into a blackened, smoldering stump.

Disgusted, Luis wrapped himself in a blanket and stood against a tree, smoking his pipe. As they slept, great feathery snowflakes drifted down from the sky. In the morning, they were covered in snow. Heads popped up through the snow and called out to one another. Quickly the group roused themselves. They asked Luis, Salvador, and Stanton if there was still time to reach the summit. But the men shook their heads. The pass was now covered by many feet of snow. The way was blocked.

The group was one day too late to reach their destination. They collected their things and pushed back to Truckee Lake. They were now trapped in the Sierra Nevada. "We had to go back," Virginia Reed remembered. "And stay there all winter."

The Sierra Nevada

CHAPTER 6
Snowed In

The snow continued to fall as the Donner Party made camp. It was now November. At Truckee Lake, the Breens moved into a simple log cabin built there years earlier. The other families felled trees to build new shelters. The Murphys constructed a cabin next to a large boulder; the Graveses and Reeds built a double cabin with a dividing wall. The Kesebergs built a lean-to against the Breens' cabin. Charles Stanton, Luis, Salvador, and the Eddys bunked with the others.

Meanwhile, the Donner family was farther behind, at Alder Creek. The axle on George Donner's wagon had broken, and he had cut his hand making a new one. The Donners began building a cabin but had to stop when the snow started falling. Now they would have to survive the winter in tents. The leaky, drafty cabins the families at Truckee Lake had built were luxurious by comparison.

Now that the two groups had shelter, most of their remaining oxen were slaughtered. Some meat was frozen in the snow, and the rest was eaten. No part of the animals was wasted: oxtails were put into soup kettles, hides were stretched over leaky cabin roofs.

Oxen meat and flour became the staple food for those families who had it. But some families had more than others. The Graveses and Breens had six oxen each, the Eddys had one, and the Reeds had none. Margaret Reed purchased two oxen from the Breens. The Graveses sold another one of the oxen to the Eddys, for twenty-five dollars.

But the animal was so thin that there was barely any meat on it. At Alder Creek, the Donners were low on food. Also, the snow kept the sides of their canvas tents constantly wet. They wore wet clothes and slept in damp beds. The relentless snow meant nothing could dry. And the snow kept coming.

Another snowstorm lasted for eight days straight. All the snowbound travelers could do was cut wood, collect snow to melt for water, and try to keep warm in bed. On November 20, Patrick Breen began a diary. For weeks, he recorded little else except details about the snowfall. On November 28, Breen wrote: "Snowing fast . . . snow 8 or 10 inches deep. Soft wet snow." On December 1: "Still snowing . . . snow about 5½ feet or 6 deep difficult to get wood no going from the house." Meanwhile, some oxen and mules had been lost in the snow. With drifts of twenty feet high, there was no way of finding them. "No living thing without wings can get about," Breen wrote.

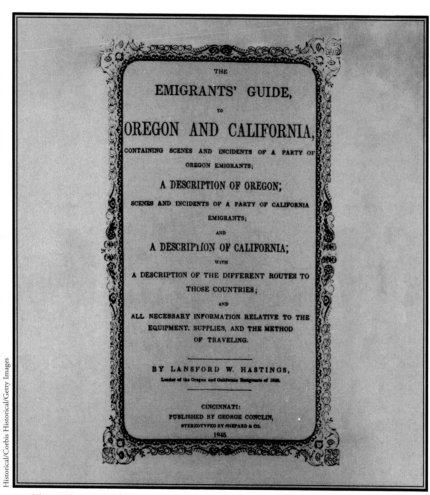

THE

EMIGRANTS' GUIDE,

TO

OREGON AND CALIFORNIA,

CONTAINING SCENES AND INCIDENTS OF A PARTY OF
OREGON EMIGRANTS;

A DESCRIPTION OF OREGON;

SCENES AND INCIDENTS OF A PARTY OF CALIFORNIA
EMIGRANTS;

AND

A DESCRIPTION OF CALIFORNIA;

WITH

A DESCRIPTION OF THE DIFFERENT ROUTES TO
THOSE COUNTRIES;

AND

ALL NECESSARY INFORMATION RELATIVE TO THE
EQUIPMENT, SUPPLIES, AND THE METHOD
OF TRAVELING.

BY LANSFORD W. HASTINGS,

Leader of the Oregon and California Emigrants of 1842.

CINCINNATI:
PUBLISHED BY GEORGE CONCLIN,
STEREOTYPED BY SHEPARD & CO.
1845.

The title page of Lansford Hastings's book, *The Emigrants' Guide to Oregon and California*

The Sierra Nevada

An example of a wagon train traveling, 1874

Fort Laramie in Wyoming, 1957

The Great Salt Lake Desert

Covered wagons create a corral to keep livestock in.

A man walks on part of Donner Pass, 1867

A bison

An illustration of the Donner Party struggling through the snow.

Donner Lake, 1910

Part of the Donner Party campsite with remaining tree stumps

DONNER CAMP

HAS BEEN DESIGNATED A
REGISTERED NATIONAL
HISTORIC LANDMARK

UNDER THE PROVISIONS OF THE
HISTORIC SITES ACT OF AUGUST 21, 1935
THIS SITE POSSESSES EXCEPTIONAL VALUE
IN COMMEMORATING AND ILLUSTRATING
THE HISTORY OF THE UNITED STATES

U.S. DEPARTMENT OF THE INTERIOR
NATIONAL PARK SERVICE

1961

A historical marker for the campsite of the Donner Party in
Truckee, California

The inside of the Donner Memorial State Park Museum

Robert Holmes/Corbis Historical/Getty Images

Tourists in front of the Pioneer Monument in Truckee, California

A portrait of Donner Party member Patty Reed next to her doll

Conditions became steadily worse. Steps had to be cut into the snow to get out of the cabins to chop wood. The green wood made the fires terribly smoky. The family members, trying to stay warm, lay beneath filthy blankets. They were covered with lice. Many went to the bathroom in a communal pot rather than go outside. The cabins and tents stank.

Most families now had little or no food. Some began boiling ox hides and bones with snow to make a type of edible paste. Others caught mice and roasted them whole over the fire. Hungrier

 people ate pieces of their own buffalo clothes. Help was needed, and fast.

On December 16, the snow finally stopped. It was a chance to escape. That morning at Truckee Lake, ten men, five women, and two boys set out on homemade snowshoes to cross the mountain. The group became known as the Forlorn Hope. They took with them precious last supplies of dried meat and coffee. However, their snowshoes were only partly effective. Most of the time, they sank into the snow with each step. It was exhausting work. After two full days, the Forlorn Hope had only gotten as far as the mountain summit.

The group struggled on for six days after eventually crossing the mountain. They were lost. Some members had snow blindness, which is caused by the sun at high altitudes. Worse still, the food rations had run out. At one point, Charles Stanton could go no farther. He sat down, lit his pipe, and said he would catch up with the others. He was not seen again.

On Christmas Day, the Forlorn Hope huddled around a fire with blankets over their heads. Around them, a snowstorm raged. If they did not eat, they would soon die. It was then that someone suggested that if they ate one of their dead companions, then the rest could survive. But no one was dead. Would one person therefore have to sacrifice themselves? How would they choose who? Because it was Christmas, the subject went no further. All the group could do was sit and look at one another. The idea of cannibalism— eating human flesh—was put aside.

A few hours later, Patrick Dolan was so desperate and overwhelmed by the situation that he tore off his clothes and ran into the snow. The group pulled him back, but it was too late, and he died. The rest of the group cut strips of his body and cooked them. As the days passed, more members of the Forlorn Hope died, and they were eaten, too. On New Year's Day, the snowstorm finally stopped. The remaining five men and five women, along with the two boys, headed out once more.

The human remains the Forlorn Hope had carried with them only lasted a few days. Starving, some members began eating the laces on their snowshoes. The subject of cannibalism resurfaced.

Luis and Salvador, the only two men who had not eaten any of the human flesh, began fearing for their lives. They slipped away from the group in the night. The others continued to argue about who could be sacrificed for food.

As the group struggled on, they found tracks leading to Luis and Salvador. The pair were alive but had collapsed against a tree. Taking a gun, William Foster shot both men. Their bodies were then cut up and distributed. This provided enough food for the Forlorn Hope to reach civilization.

On January 17, William Eddy reached Johnson's Ranch, California. The daughter of the rancher, Harriet Ritchie, opened the door to Eddy. Filthy, skeletal, and with feet bloody from frostbite, he asked for bread. At the sight of Eddy, Harriet burst into tears. She put him to bed and raised the alarm to others at Johnson's Ranch.

By following Eddy's bloody footprints, ranch hands found the other members of the Forlorn Hope farther up the trail. Five women and two men had survived. Their journey from Truckee Lake had taken them thirty-three days.

CHAPTER 7
Relief Parties

When William Eddy became strong enough to talk, he told a terrible tale of starvation, madness, and cannibalism. Even worse, most of the Donner Party was still stuck in the Sierra Nevada. Word was quickly sent to Sutter's Fort. A group of rescuers—called the First Relief Party—was put together. Just behind it, a second relief party had already set out from Sutter's Fort. Its leader was James Reed.

After being banished from the Donner Party for killing John Snyder, Reed had reached Sutter's Fort. He had attempted to put together a supply train and head back toward the Sierra Nevada. But the snow had stopped him passing. When the Mexican-American War broke out, all able-bodied men in California were called on to fight. There was no one left to help with his rescue mission. In January 1847, the men were released from fighting the war, and on January 31, James Reed was able to ride out at the head of the Second Relief Party.

The First Relief Party arrived at Truckee Lake on February 18. They could see smoke rising from the ground but no camp. After the rescuers shouted out "hallo," a gaunt figure appeared through a hole in the snow. It was Levinah Murphy. "Are you men from California or do you come from heaven?" she asked in an agitated voice.

The conditions of the camp shocked the rescuers. Dead bodies lay on the snow, some covered in quilts. In the cabins, pots contained the gluey mixture of boiled ox hides and bones. An overpowering stench was everywhere. The survivors were so weak, many could not stand.

Levinah Murphy

The Mexican-American War

The Mexican-American War began over a border dispute in the Republic of Texas, over land that had once belonged to Mexico but had become independent in 1836. Mexico wanted Texas to remain a part of Mexico, while the United States wanted the republic to join the Union as a new state. The war lasted from

1846 to 1848. During that time, the United States also conquered the Mexican territory of California.

The war ended with the 1848 Treaty of Guadalupe Hidalgo. The United States gained more than five hundred thousand square miles of land for a $15 million payment to Mexico. The land from the treaty is now made up of the modern states of California, Nevada, Arizona, Utah, and parts of Oklahoma, Wyoming, Colorado, and New Mexico.

Farther down the mountain at Alder Creek, the Donners were in an even worse state. George Donner's hand was now too infected to use. Tamzene Donner refused to leave his side.

The First Relief Party left a limited amount of supplies with the Donners. They then collected twenty-three people from both camps for the journey back to Johnson's Ranch. Among those being rescued was Margaret Reed. After the group passed the summit, they met the Second Relief Party. Margaret nearly fainted with joy at the sound of her husband's voice. Later, he remembered the sight of the starving families: "I cannot describe the death-like look of them. 'Bread, bread, bread' was the begging of every child and grown person."

After the meeting, the Second Relief Party pressed on to Truckee Lake and Alder Creek. Here, only a week had passed since the First Relief Party had left. But things were much worse. Some of the pioneers had resorted to cannibalism to survive. It was the only thing that was preventing the Donner children from starving. Two days later, Reed and the Second Relief Party led seventeen people over the mountain pass. The rest were too weak to move and waited for the Third Relief Party.

For those leaving, however, escape was not so simple. After crossing the peak and traveling down the other side, another snowstorm struck. This blizzard was so bad that the group had no choice but to build a fire and wait it out. The fire had to be built on green branches laid across the snow. But soon, the snow melted and the fire sank. The group were left in a pit, surrounded by walls of snow.

Before long, those in the pit began dying from starvation. They became known as the Starved Camp. Those living were too weak to do anything but wait for death or a relief party. James Reed, however, would not wait. He pleaded with the others to move on. When they would not, Reed put his daughter on his back and left toward Sutter's Fort.

Five days later, the Third Relief Party, led by William Eddy and William Foster, stumbled upon the Starved Camp. The sight horrified them.

On the snow above the pit lay three butchered bodies. In the pit below were eleven pioneers, all starving and unable to move. The Third Relief Party then split into two: three men stayed to help the Starved Camp to safety, while Eddy and Foster kept going to Truckee Lake. Incredibly, the eleven Starved Camp survivors all made it to safety and lived to tell the tale.

Eddy and Foster had both left their children at Truckee Lake. But when they returned on March 14, they found that they all had died. Worse still, Lewis Keseberg admitted that he had eaten their remains. After threatening to kill Keseberg, Eddy and Foster left with most of the last survivors. Keseberg and Tamzene Donner stayed behind. Although her husband, George, was close to death, Tamzene stayed with him.

In April, a Fourth Relief Party arrived at Truckee Lake. The group was surprised to find

Lewis Keseberg still alive in one of the cabins. After much questioning, Keseberg admitted to eating the body of Tamzene Donner. He said Tamzene had come to his cabin after George had died. Keseberg said that she died during the night. The rescuers suspected Keseberg had killed and eaten Tamzene. They then found he had stolen some of the Donners' possessions, including $250 in gold.

The rescuers marched Keseberg from the Truckee Lake location.

When the Fourth Relief Party reached Johnson's Ranch with Keseberg, the rescue was complete. Eighty-nine people had been trapped in the Sierra Nevada. Forty-two had died, and forty-seven had survived. The Donner Party's journey was finally over.

CHAPTER 8
History Remembers

It took a long time for members of the Donner Party to recover from their terrible ordeal. In the warm spring air, Virginia Reed wrote to her cousin in Illinois. She mentioned putting on weight—"we are all very fleshy"—and living in California. "It is a beautiful country. It ought to be a beautiful country to pay us for our trouble getting there."

Slowly, the survivors began their new lives in California. Few who had traveled west in the Donner Party ever saw one another again. The Reed family settled in San Jose. There, James Reed made a fortune in real estate. Margaret Reed stopped having headaches. The Breens settled in San Juan Bautista, where they became ranchers.

William Eddy remarried and began a new family. Lewis Keseberg's reputation as a "man-eater" followed him for the rest of his life. He died in the 1890s, penniless and homeless, in a hospital for the poor.

The Murphy, Donner, and Graves children were all made orphans by the tragedy in the Sierra Nevada. Some of the Donner children were taken in by the Reeds; others were adopted by other Californian families. Years later, Eliza Donner talked about her experiences in a memoir called *The Expedition of the Donner Party and Its Tragic Fate*. Nancy Graves, by comparison, was haunted by the memory of the cannibalism. She refused to talk about it.

The fact that they had eaten some of

their companions was headline news after the last survivors of the Donner Party escaped the mountain. Some newspapers played down the cannibalism; others exaggerated it. It has been the subject of debate and fascination ever since. It is the reason the Donner Party is still talked and written about.

Today, many Donner Party members are also remembered for their bravery. After all, they were everyday people who had to make the hardest of decisions in the face of great danger. In the end, their will to survive overcame all else. And their story is only one of many among the thousands of people who traveled west to carve out a better life for themselves.

It is possible to visit Truckee Lake in California, which has been renamed Donner Memorial State Park. Stores, hotels, restaurants, and a major highway are only a few minutes away.

On quiet, snowy days, it is still possible to imagine what it was like more than 176 years ago at Truckee Lake, as snowstorms struck and the mountain summit became impassable. We can hope that we would have energy enough for one last push over the summit before it became blocked. And we can think of Virginia Reed's advice to her cousin after surviving the ordeal: "Never take no cutoffs and hurry along as fast as you can."

Donner Memorial State Park

In 1918, a "Pioneer Monument" honoring the Donner Party was erected at Truckee Lake, where the Breen cabin had stood. The monument consists of a bronze statue of a pioneer family atop a twenty-two-foot stone pedestal. The three figures are all gazing west, toward California.

In 1928, the region around Truckee Lake and Alder Creek was turned into Donner Memorial State Park. Today, visitors to the park can have a guided tour of the sites where the Donner Party cabins stood and visit the Donner Memorial State Park Visitor Center. Newly renovated in 2015, the center has exhibits about the Donner Party and other pioneers who were part of America's Westward Expansion.